PARK LANE COLLEGE
HORSFORTH CENTRE LIBRARY
Calverley Lane, Horsforth, Leeds LS18 4RQ Tel: 2162440

This book must be returned by the latest date shown.
Please bring the book with you or telephone if you wish
to extend the period of loan. Short loan books are not
renewable.

FINES WILL BE CHARGED ON OVERDUE BOOKS.

MILESTONES
IN MODERN SCIENCE

THE FIRST
COMPUTERS

Guy de la Bédoyère

Evans

Published by Evans Brothers Limited
2A Portman Mansions
Chiltern Street
London W1U 6NR

British Library Cataloguing in Publication Data

De la Bedoyere, Guy
The first computers. - (Milestones in modern science)
    1. Computers – History - Juvenile literature
    2. Discoveries in science - Juvenile literature
    I. Title
004

ISBN 0237527413

Consultant: Dr Anne Whitehead
Editor: Sonya Newland
Designer: D.R. Ink, info@d-r-ink.com
Picture researcher: Julia Bird

Acknowledgements

Cover Science Photo Library; Laguna Design/Science Photo Library; Volker Steger/Science Photo Library 3 Tek Image/Science Photo Library 4 Science Museum/Science & Society Picture Library 5 Will & Deni McIntyre/Science Photo Library 6 Antonia Reeve/Science Photo Library 7(t) Laguna Design/Science Photo Library 7(b) Ferranti Electronics/A. Sternberg/Science Photo Library 8 Jerry Mason/Science Photo Library 10(t) © Ed Young/Corbis 10(b) © Charles & Josette Lenars/Corbis 11 © Araido de Luca/Corbis 12(t) J-L Charmet/Science Photo Library 12(b) David Parker/Science Photo Library 13 Dr Jeremy Burgess/Science Photo Library 15 J-L Charmet/Science Photo Library 16 Science Photo Library 17(t) Science Museum/Science & Society Picture Library 17(b) Science Photo Library 18 Science Museum/Science & Society Picture Library 19 Science Museum/Science & Society Picture Library 20(l) © Bettmann/Corbis 20(r) Science Museum/Science & Society Picture Library 21(t) J-L Charmet/Science Photo Library 22 Volker Steger/Science Photo Library 23(t) Science Photo Library 23(b) Science Photo Library 24(t) James King-Holmes/Bletchley Park Trust/Science Photo Library 24(b) Science Museum/Science & Society Picture Library 25 Science Photo Library 26 Alfred Pasieka/Science Photo Library 27(t) © Bettmann/Corbis 27(b) Science Museum/Science & Society Picture Library 28(t) Bletchley Park Trust/Science & Society Picture Library 28(b) Science Photo Library 29 Volker Steger/Science Photo Library 30(l) Science Museum/Science & Society Picture Library 30(r) Bletchley Park Trust/Science & Society Picture Library 31 Los Alamos National Laboratory/Science Photo Library 32 Science Museum/Science & Society Picture Library 33 © Bettmann/Corbis 34(b) © Bettmann/Corbis 35(t) Sheila Terry/Rutherford Appleton Laboratory/Science Photo Library 35(b) Tony Craddock/Science Photo Library 36(t) Simon Fraser/Science Photo Library 36(b) © Jim Sugar/Corbis 37 Science Museum/Science & Society Picture Library 38 Peter Menzel/Science Photo Library 39(t) Science Museum/Science & Society Picture Library 39(b) Peter Menzel/Science Photo Library 40(t) Samuel Ashfield/Science Photo Library 40(b) Simon Fraser/Science Photo Library 41 Gusto/Science Photo Library 42 David Parker/Science Photo Library 43 Simon Fraser/Science Photo Library 44 © Bettmann/Corbis

CONTENTS

'Never before in history has innovation offered promise of so much to so many in so short a time.' **BILL GATES, FOUNDER OF MICROSOFT**

Introduction

ABOVE: *In 1948, when the Manchester Mark I (pictured) was built, computers were enormous – often taking up a whole room or more. Programming and using them was extremely complicated. Within just a few years, all that had changed.*

In 1968, when the Apollo space missions began, the heart of the mission-control centre in Houston was five IBM (International Business Machines Corporation) computers. Each one was the size of a small car and had a total memory capacity of one megabyte. At the time, this was the cutting edge of technology. It is amazing to think that today, a mobile phone that can fit in the palm of one hand has more than twice the memory capacity of one of those computers that helped to put a man on the Moon.

This great leap – from enormous computers used by only a few government organisations and industries for the most complicated tasks, to machines that have infiltrated almost every aspect of our everyday lives – has taken place in less than a lifetime. People who began working in the new computer industry in the 1960s may well still be in that industry today, and the changes they have seen are extraordinary.

Before this time, everything that we now take for granted as the function of a computer was carried out by people. Certainly some inventors created basic machines that would assist them, but by and large they had to rely on hard work and intelligence. It was not only time-consuming, but also, on occasion, impossible. In the second half of the twentieth century, computer technology took off in a way that no one could have expected or foreseen.

There is no doubt that computers revolutionised the world. They have contributed to the massive leap in efficiency in trade and industry; they have radically changed accepted methods of communication; they have opened up a whole new world of information that is cheap and accessible to almost everyone. Everything is faster, better, more effective. Indeed the influence of computers has affected just about every area of our lives.

Today, different elements of computer technology have been adapted for extremely diverse purposes. Thanks to computers, forensic scientists have been able to use DNA testing to solve crimes committed decades ago. In medical science, computers are used for researching cures for diseases that have previously been untreatable. In hospitals, computer technology is used in all electrical equipment for monitoring patients, and for treatments such as radiation therapy. Thanks to modern technology, we can track parcels from one side of the globe to the other and have instant access, via the Internet, to knowledge about where it is at any precise moment, what time it reaches its destination, and even who signs the delivery note at the other end. In the simplest ways, that we hardly even notice, we use computers every day – through automated services such as cash machines or chip-and-pin methods of payment in shops and restaurants. We live in a world of instant communication – written, verbal and visual, through mobile phones, email and instant messenging – and instant information, through the World Wide Web.

But where did it this amazing technology come from? How did the world move from using simple calculating implements like the abacus to machines that can work out immensely complex mathematics in the blink of an eye? There were many people involved, each of whom built on previous knowledge and added a little of their own resourcefulness. As well as this, many developments were made more or less simultaneously in different countries. As such, there are differences in opinion about what exactly was the very first computer, and there are many machines that could claim the title. Nonetheless, the history of the computer is a fascinating story of trial and error, necessity, failure, determination and – more than anything – human ingenuity.

RIGHT: Computers just keep getting smaller. Today, some are so small they can fit in your pocket and be carried anywhere you go.

CHAPTER ONE

'You can't just ask customers what they want and then try to give that to them. By the time you get it built, they'll want something new.' **STEVEN JOBS, CEO OF APPLE COMPUTERS**

Computers Today

ABOVE: *Many people have computers like this one – a standard PC – in their homes, and use them for work, playing games and surfing the Internet.*

LIKE MOST LIFE-CHANGING INVENTIONS, the computer was the product of many years of design and inspiration from many different people – from their very beginnings as simple mechanical calculators to the multi-purpose machines that are now an intrinsic part of our world. To really realise the enormity of this achievement, it is important to understand today's computers, and the amazing technology that has made them such a significant part of our everyday lives.

PARTS OF A COMPUTER

A desktop computer has several external components, or parts, all joined together with cables. (In a laptop computer, all these parts are contained in a portable case.) The mouse and the keyboard are called 'input' devices. The screen is where the computer displays the information that is put into it, and is an 'output' device.

The computer itself is the large box. Inside the box there is a circuit board – the motherboard. The motherboard sorts out what is typed in, what is clicked with the

Fact

WHAT IS A MICROPROCESSOR?

A microprocessor is the heart of most computers — a single chip where all the information is translated and sent out again. When talking about personal computers people tend to use the words 'microprocessor' and 'CPU' to mean the same thing. Micro-processors are used to interpret and process data in all kinds of machines, from clock radios to cars.

ABOVE: Microprocessor chips, like this Ferranti F100-L, are so tiny they can fit in the eye of a needle, yet they contain the complex technology that controls all the functions of a computer.

mouse and the programs that are running. In the middle of the motherboard is the Central Processing Unit (CPU). This is the microprocessor that does all the hard work. Data is carried through the motherboard to the CPU, which translates it and works out what information needs to be sent where. The motherboard then sends signals to the screen and to the speakers, so the user can see and hear the results of the instructions to the computer.

MEMORY

Computers have three different types of memory:

Random Access Memory (RAM): This is a temporary memory, and although it is very fast, it only works when the computer is switched on. The processor uses RAM to store information it is working on at a particular time. If the computer is turned off, everything in the RAM is instantly forgotten.

Read Only Memory (ROM): This is stored in a chip on the motherboard and contains the information about the computer itself – what programs are available and what equipment is fitted.

Hard drive: This is the permanent memory, where all the programs, documents, photographs, and other information are stored, even when the computer is switched off. Hard-drive memory is bigger than RAM, but it is much slower.

As well as a hard drive, computers have other drives that can read information stored on disks like floppy disks (small disks that can hold around 1 megabyte of information), CDs and DVDs. These additional drives have motors in them to spin the disks, while special heads read the data and send it down a ribbon cable to the motherboard.

BELOW: As well as the main hard drive of the computer, there are different types of external hard drive that can be attached. These read information from disks and sent it down wires to the motherboard. External hard drives include (from top to bottom) Zip drive, external hard disk, CD-Rom player, SyQuest drive and floppy disk drive.

WHAT IS A PROGRAM?

Programs are the instructions the computer follows in order to function. They let the user write things, play games or make music. The most important program on any computer is the operating system (OS). This is a kind of language or set of rules, and the computer cannot work without it. Today, the most widely used operating system is Microsoft Windows. The operating system creates an 'environment' in which other programs can work. It also makes sure these other programs can work together, i.e. that they are compatible. One of the main problems with early computers was that programs for one computer did not work on another.

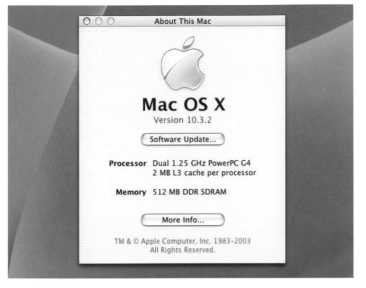

LEFT: *OS X (OS Ten) is the latest operating system from Apple Computer. Operating systems are the programs on computers that allow other programs or applications to run. They are constantly being updated and newer, more efficient versions are regularly available.*

Fact

COMPUTER EQUIPMENT

MODEMS send the computer's data down a telephone line, or receive information the same way and send it into the computer. DIGITAL CAMERAS can send their pictures through a cable into the computer. SCANNERS turn printed photographs or pages of text into data and send them into the computer. PRINTERS are where the computer sends the finished work to be printed out. The printed work is called a hard copy.

BELOW: *Information is sent down cables from the keyboard and mouse, as well as other external equipment such as hard drives. The information travels through the motherboard to the CPU, where it is processed and sent back via the motherboard to output devices like the screen and printer. The memory chips sit on the motherboard and information is sent between them and the CPU.*

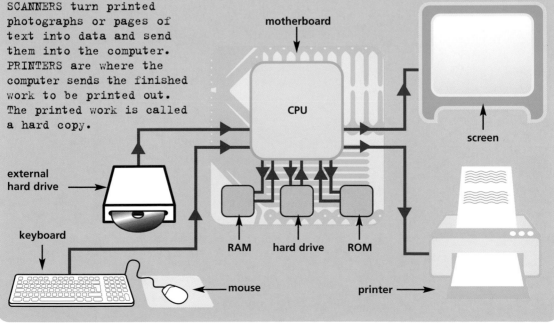

CHAPTER TWO

'Expressing every possible number using a set of ten symbols ... seems so simple nowadays that its ... profound importance is no longer appreciated.' **PIERRE-SIMON LAPLACE, EIGHTEENTH-CENTURY MATHEMATICIAN**

Ancient World to New Science

ABOVE: *Abacuses were some of the earliest calculating devices, and were used in many ancient civilisations.*

BELOW: *In Mesopotamia, data was recorded on stone tablets using characters called cuneiform. This tablet was discovered in the ancient city of Ugarit, and dates from around 1400 BC.*

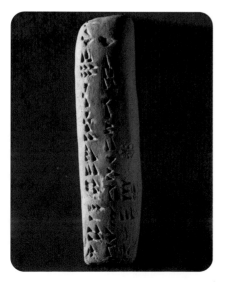

ALL THE KEY ELEMENTS OF COMPUTERS discussed in the previous chapter are largely the result of great leaps in understanding technology that occurred in the second half of the twentieth century. Today's computers can process more data in a few seconds than a mathematical genius could manage in a lifetime, and it took a very long time for these machines to become so advanced. However, many of the ideas used in making the modern computer have been around for thousands of years.

EARLY WAYS OF PROCESSING INFORMATION

'Compute' simply means 'count'. Counting with ten fingers is the basis of the decimal system. Other ways of recording simple mathematical information included cutting notches into sticks or using pebbles. This may seem obvious, but it was the only way early humans had of keeping records of their cattle and other possessions. In ancient times, pebbles were used to create the first reliable calculating machine – the abacus.

Abacus is the Latin word for a flat surface. Stones were laid out in rows of ten; later the stones were drilled and strung on cords in a wooden frame. Counting was simple – in a Chinese abacus (pictured left), each of the beads above the crossbar represented five units and each bead below the crossbar one unit. The first column on the right represented ones, the second on the right tens, the third hundreds, and so on. An experienced abacus-user could add and subtract huge numbers very quickly and accurately. Abacuses like this remained in use right up until the modern electronic calculator was created.

The first certain evidence of recording information appeared in Mesopotamia (modern Iraq) in about 3500 BC. Wedge-shaped characters called cuneiform were made on wet clay tablets; once baked and hardened, the tablets held a permanent record of data. In ancient Egypt, from about 2500 BC, certain hieroglyphs (the Egyptian form of writing using symbols based on animals, people, gods and implements) represented numbers, and were used to record dates and quantities.

By about 500 BC, the ancient Greeks were beginning to develop more sophisticated mathematics. Early mathematicians, such as Pythagoras and Euclid, worked out many basic laws of geometry. The principles of mathematics established by the Greeks were developed further by the Romans from around the first century AD.

THE ARABIC SYSTEM

In seventh-century India, a system was devised using symbols to represent numbers. These symbols were 0, 1, 2, 3, 4, 5, 6, 7, 8, 9. Each of these symbols had an 'absolute value' and a 'place value'. Take the numeral '2' as an example. On its own '2' represents the number two. This is its absolute value. When written in another number, though, for example '23', the character '2' now represents the number 20. In the number 234, '2' represents 200. The 'meaning' of the symbol changes depending on where in the number it appears. This is its

***ABOVE:** This stone carving is an ancient timetable, showing the market times in imperial Rome, using Roman numerals.*

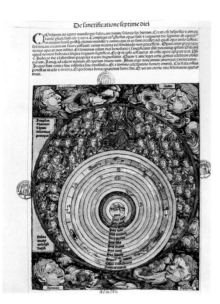

ABOVE: *In the Middle Ages, people believed in the system devised by Ptolemy (shown here in an engraving from 1493), in which the Sun and all the planets revolved around the Earth.*

BELOW: *Astrolabes were marked with angular measurements; by aligning the astrolabe with the horizon, astronomers could work out the heights and positions of the stars, which allowed them to tell the time.*

place value. This way of using numerals made addition, subtraction, multiplication and division much easier.

This, of course, is the basis of our modern system, but it was not widely known until the Arab world started to use it around the eleventh century, and because of this it is known as the Arabic system. From there it gradually spread to Europe, and by the fifteenth century it was the standard way of writing numbers.

Other civilisations had different methods of calculation. As late as the 1400s, for example, the Inca in South America were using a device similar to an abacus, called a quipus. This was a series of knotted strings. Knots represented units or multiples of ten depending on where on the string they were placed – the closer to the top, the higher the number. The highest number was 10,000 and the lowest, one. The Inca even used this device to send information between villages; the colour of the strings represented the items that were being counted – yellow was used for gold, red for the army etc.

THE MIDDLE AGES

By the fifteenth century a new science was sweeping across Europe – astronomy. For centuries people had studied the phases of the Moon and the positions of the stars, trying to work out their place in the Universe. Up until this time, people had believed that the Earth was the centre of the Universe, and that the Sun moved around it. In the early sixteenth century Nicolas Copernicus (1473–1543) claimed that the opposite was true – that the Earth was actually a planet orbiting the Sun. The mathematical calculations and closer observation he needed, though, were too complicated and he could not prove his theory.

The invention of the telescope at the end of the sixteenth century made closer examination of the heavens possible, and the Italian astronomer and mathematician Galileo Galilei

(1564–1642) used the new instrument to watch the movement of the Sun and the Moon. He announced that Copernicus had been correct.

The problem with all this was that there were no precise calculations to prove the observations. Without these, scientists and astronomers could only roughly predict where the stars and other planets would be in the sky at a point in the future.

LAWS OF PHYSICS

It was the brilliant German mathematician Johannes Kepler (1571–1630) who finally proved that Copernicus and Galileo were right. He saw that the planets orbit the Sun in ellipses (elongated circles), and from this he devised a set of 'rules' by which the planets moved. In 1627 Kepler published his astronomical tables. In England, half a century later, Isaac Newton (1642–1727) proposed his universal laws of motion and gravity – these are now the basis of modern physics. Newton and the German mathematician Gottfried Wilhelm Leibniz (1646–1716) both independently invented a system called differential calculus. This made it possible to predict the position of a planet at a given time. Leibniz went on to publish his ideas about binary numbers, believing they represented a pure form of logic. Binary code is used by all modern computers.

Mathematicians like Kepler, Leibniz and Newton opened the door to new questions about astronomy, engineering and science. Finding the answers to these questions meant doing complicated calculations that were impossible for any person to do in a lifetime. People began experimenting with machines that might help them.

ABOVE: *Gottfried Wilhelm Leibniz was the first person to publish ideas about binary numbers (the use of only two digits put into sequences to represent other numbers). Binary is the code used in all computers today.*

BINARY CODE

Computers can only tell the difference between 'on' and 'off', so all the information put into them has to be turned into long streams of 'on' and 'off' information. This is known as binary or digital code. Binary is made of two digits called 'bits': 0 and 1. The computer understands these as 'off' (0) and 'on' (1).

To see how binary works, take the number 137 as an example. The 1 represents 100 (hundreds), the 3 represents 30 (tens), and the 7 represents 7 (units). In binary, the numbers double from right to left. This table shows how decimal and binary numbers correspond:

DECIMAL	BINARY 128	64	32	16	8	4	2	1
0								0
1								1
2							1	0
3							1	1
4						1	0	0
5						1	0	1
6						1	1	0
7						1	1	1
8					1	0	0	0
9					1	0	0	1
10					1	0	1	0
11					1	0	1	1
12					1	1	0	0
13					1	1	0	1
14					1	1	1	0
15					1	1	1	1
16				1	0	0	0	0
17				1	0	0	0	1
18				1	0	0	1	0
19				1	0	0	1	1
20				1	0	1	0	0

and so on

100	0	1	1	0	0	1	0	0
137	1	0	0	0	1	0	0	1

NEW WAYS OF CALCULATING

At the beginning of the seventeenth century, several new methods of calculating were invented. The first of these became known as Napier's Bones, after its inventor John Napier (1550–1617). These were numerical tables on strips of wood or bone, each inscribed with numbers in ten squares. By placing the strips in different orders, complex multiplication could be worked out. It was still time-consuming, though, because the numbers from the different rows had to be added together before the final answer was reached. In 1621, a mathematician named William Oughtred (1574–1660) improved on Napier's Bones and created a device called a slide rule, which moved the numbers next to each other into different positions, making multiplication and division much simpler.

THE FIRST MECHANICAL CALCULATORS

The French mathematician Blaise Pascal (1623–62) was one of the first to create a calculating machine. His father was a tax collector, and part of his job was to add up long lists of numbers. This was often very complicated and time consuming, so, when he was only 18 years old, Pascal designed a mechanical calculator to help. It had eight dials on it, so it could add up numbers up to eight figures long. When the first dial (representing ones) was moved ten notches, the second dial (representing tens) would move on one

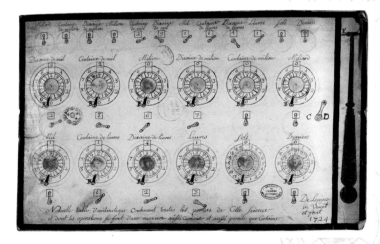

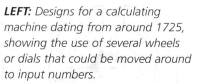

LEFT: Designs for a calculating machine dating from around 1725, showing the use of several wheels or dials that could be moved around to input numbers.

Key People

Charles Babbage (1791–1871) was an English mathematician and inventor. In the early nineteenth century, multiplication and division were usually calculated using mathematical charts called logarithmic tables. These tables were created by teams of mathematicians. Babbage was frustrated by how long it took to create the tables manually, and decided to build a machine that would make the calculations automatically. He designed several of these, including the Analytical Engine and the Difference Engine. Unfortunately, the technology of the time was not very advanced, and although Babbage began to construct his machines, none was completed. Part of the Analytical Engine was eventually finished by Babbage's son, but it turned out that it made some errors. In 1991 Babbage's Difference Engine was built at the Science Museum in London – it worked. Babbage also worked out a method of mathematical code-breaking, which would inspire computer development during the Second World War.

notch, and when that second dial had moved ten notches, the third dial (representing hundreds) would move on one notch, and so on. The problem with Pascal's machine was that it could only add or subtract, so more complicated calculations were very difficult.

In 1671, Leibniz made a more sophisticated decimal calculator. This had a special wheel with cogs on it, called a stepped drum, which processed data. It could add, subtract, divide and multiply. More than 250 years later, mechanical calculating machines still used similar techniques. Eight years after creating his decimal calculator Leibniz drew up plans for a calculating machine that used binary code.

The problem with these early machines was that they were large and slow. More significantly, they had no memory. All the data had to be entered by hand, and results had to be written down as they could not be stored in the machine. Mistakes were easy to make.

So, people began looking for ways of storing information on machines. In the early eighteenth century, weaving and cloth-making were important industries and it was here that the first mechanical storage systems were created. The machines used for making cloth used a device called a drawboy. This ran thread through the fabric in a particular way for each design. It was not always accurate and a single mistake could ruin the pattern on the cloth. In 1804, the French weaver Joseph Marie Jacquard (1752–1834) developed a way of storing the pattern data on punched wooden cards. These cards controlled how the weave was made, and a different card was used for each pattern. At last a way had been found to record and reuse data. When the first real computers were built more than a century later they used this method to store information.

LEFT: The Jacquard loom used perforated wooden cards to store information about different patterns. A series of connected cards were passed over the needles in the loom. When a hole came up, the needle would go through it, activating the threading mechanism. The pattern of holes on the card determined the pattern on the cloth. By storing the pattern data in this way, Jacquard ensured that no mistakes were made, and he could recreate the same pattern in exactly the same way any time he wanted.

Fact

THE ANALYTICAL ENGINE

Babbage's Analytical Engine has often been called the first computer. It was designed in 1833, and used Jacquard's device of punched cards to input and store information. It was programmable, had a memory, and used array processing, in which different pieces of data are organised in a series and their locations remembered (a format still used today). Babbage was helped in his design by Ada Byron, Lady Lovelace (1815–52), who wrote to Babbage with several programs that would process information in the Analytical Engine. Lady Lovelace might be considered to be the first computer programmer.

RIGHT: Charles Babbage's Analytical Engine used the system of punched cards devised by Jacquard to store and input information.

CHAPTER THREE

'I never did anything by accident, nor did any of my inventions come by accident; they came by hard work.'

AMERICAN INVENTOR THOMAS EDISON

Electricity, Vacuum Tubes and New Visions

ABOVE: *The French engineer Emile Baudot invented a communications system using binary code, as well as the hardware used to send it. Six operators were able to send messages using the same line. This picture shows a station and operators working with Baudot's system.*

AS THE NINETEENTH CENTURY PROGRESSED science entered a whole new era. Many discoveries were made and new questions were raised. Mathematics began to play an important role not just in science, but also in engineering, navigation and trade. But still the only way to do this mathematics was on paper, using complicated tables. People began to work on developing the machines that had been invented in the previous two centuries.

THE WORLD CHANGES

One of the first effective practical applications of binary code was a machine invented in 1874 by the French telegraph engineer Emile Baudot (1845–1903). He got the idea from the system of Morse code, which had been in use since the telegraph was invented in 1837. In Morse code, all the letters in a message were translated into a series of short and long electrical pulses (dots and dashes). They were sent through a telegraph wire and an operator at the other end would translate the dots and dashes back into letters and numbers. The problem

Fact

KELVIN'S TIDE PREDICTOR

The tide predictor was one of the first machines to make mechanical calculations and print out the results on paper. It was invented in 1876 by William Thomson, Lord Kelvin (1824-1907) and used a system of pulleys and gears that sketched the rise and fall of the tides on a rotating drum. All that Kelvin needed to do was input information about the position of the Sun and the Moon in relation to a particular point on the Earth. Obviously, this machine was invented for a specific purpose and only had one use, but Kelvin knew that if he built a much bigger machine along similar lines, it could compute much more complex calculations. Unfortunately, like Babbage's, Kelvin's designs were so advanced that the machine could not be built.

RIGHT: *The tide predictor had ten dials that were set with astronomical data from a particular point in a harbour. The handle was then cranked and the machine calculated the tidal patterns that would occur for up to a year in that harbour. The calculations took around four hours to make.*

with this was that the operators at each end of the telegraph had to know Morse code perfectly, and different characters took different lengths of time to send.

Baudot's machine turned a message into binary code. Every letter or number was represented by a special code made of five units, using dots and the letter X. For example, the letter A was ..X.. and the letter B was .X..X; the operator used a special five-key keyboard to enter the five units of each character at the same time. For an X the key was left up; for a dot (.) the key was depressed. The units were put in all at once, and the machine turned each dot into an off-signal (0) and each X into an on-signal (1), and sent the data down the line. At the other end another machine heard the stream of 0s and 1s and decoded them back into characters so that the message could be read.

THE FIRST ELECTRICAL MACHINES

In the late nineteenth century America's population grew rapidly as millions of immigrants arrived from Europe. A census was held every ten years to count the

Fact

HARNESSING ELECTRICITY

Since ancient times, people had known that static electricity existed, but until the nineteenth century no one had worked out a way to harness or store it, so it could not be used as a power source. In 1831 Michael Faraday (1791–1867) made the first dynamo, a device that converted mechanical energy into electrical energy. Within 50 years of this, electricity was being generated for public use, and Hollerith was one of the first to take advantage of it, with his census-counting machine.

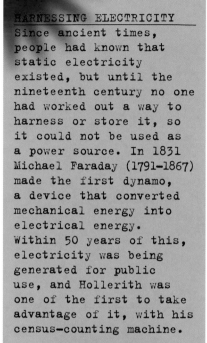

ABOVE: *The dynamo was a device that could turn mechanical energy into electrical energy.*

RIGHT: *Hollerith's machine was a mechanical system for recording data using Jacquard's punched-card method. At first there were three separate machines – a punch, a sorter and a tabulator (pictured) – but he later combined these three into one machine.*

population. It was a huge job, however, and by 1887 government officials still had not finished counting the 1880 census! There was obviously an urgent need for more sophisticated calculating machines.

The problem was solved by Herman Hollerith (1860–1929). He devised a system using punched cards. A card represented one household. On the card, holes were punched to show where the family came from, how many children there were, and other information required in the census. The cards were put into a machine that detected the holes and then totalled the results for each category. Hollerith's census-counting machine could not store data, and all it did was add up figures that would previously have been written down and added by hand; however, it processed information much faster than a person could. Most importantly – at least in terms of how later computing machines developed – Hollerith's machine was electrical. Without electricity, modern computers simply could not exist.

The census-counting machine was so successful that in 1896 Hollerith formed his own company to try to invent other machines. In 1911 he joined up with two other companies to make a new firm, later called International Business Machines. IBM was the first company set up to investigate computer technology, and it is still doing so today.

THE VACUUM TUBE

Hollerith was not the only person to realise how useful electricity could be when devising machines. Many scientists and inventors began experimenting with electricity to find out exactly what it could do. The American inventor Thomas Edison (1847–1931) was fascinated by electricity and conducted several experiments to harness its properties. On one occasion he was passing an electric current through a metal filament in an evacuated glass tube, when he noticed a curious effect. If he put a metal plate inside the tube, the electric current jumped from the filament to the plate. He called this the 'Edison Effect'. Although Edison himself could not see a use for this strange phenomenon, other scientists experimented further to see if the effect could be put to any practical use.

One of these scientists was Lee De Forest (1873–1961). De Forest was trying to find a way of picking up radio signals so that less powerful and cheaper transmitters could be used. He harnessed the

34_La lampe à arc.

ABOVE: *Of all Thomas Edison's many inventions, the light bulb is the best known and had the most impact on everyday life. This illustration, dating from 1910, celebrates its invention.*

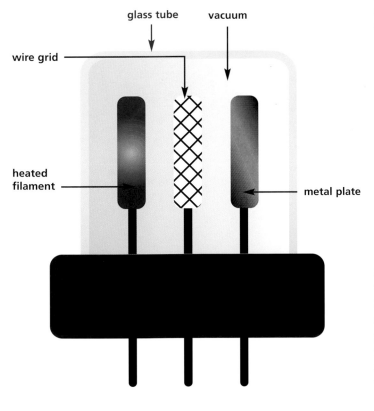

glass tube   vacuum

wire grid

heated filament

metal plate

LEFT: *Lee De Forest created the vacuum tube – an early form of the transistor – by placing a wire grid between a filament and a metal plate in a vacuum. The grid effectively controlled the electric current flowing from the filament to the plate, and worked well as an amplifier.*

RIGHT: Vacuum tubes like these, from the Johnniac mainframe computer built in 1953, were used as switching devices to turn electricity on and off in early computing machines.

Edison Effect and discovered that if he sent radio signals along a nickel wire (the grid) inside the tube, the current jumping from filament to plate amplified the radio signals. These tubes with wire inside them became known as vacuum tubes. They could also act as valves, or switches, to control the flow of electricity in a circuit; because of this, they could be connected together to process the electrical signals used in computers. They were efficient and reliable as long as they were left switched on, but they burnt out quickly if they were turned on and off. Using electricity like this was a great step towards the development of modern computers.

INTO THE MODERN AGE OF COMPUTING

In 1930, at the Massachusetts Institute of Technology in the United States, Vannevar Bush built a new type of calculating machine. He called it his differential analyser, and it seemed to be based on Lord Kelvin's plans for a larger version of his tide predictor. Bush denied he had copied Kelvin's design, but apart from his use of vacuum tubes, the two machines showed remarkable similarities.

The vacuum tubes in the differential analyser were used to create a memory, storing parts of the calculation as they were made. For the first time, a machine could remember the information put into it, and recall that information when it was needed. Bush's computer was so successful that from 1935 the US Ordnance Department used it to calculate the path of shells fired from weapons. There were still problems with the machine. It was very large – about 15 m long – and it was extremely complicated to use. For every calculation made, parts of the computer had to be moved around, and it often broke down. The problems this created led to a new generation of computers built during the Second World War.

Key People

Vannevar Bush (1890–1974) was an American scientist who bridged the gap between the days of early mechanical computing machines and modern electric computers. His differential analyser was large and complicated to use, but it opened people's eyes to the possibilities that could be offered by this new technology. Bush was a great innovator; he anticipated the Internet with his idea of Memex, which he imagined as an instant-access knowledge storehouse of text and images, organised in a format that everyone would be able to use. Memex stimulated the creators of hypertext, the language in which all Internet pages are now written.

CHAPTER FOUR

'Machines take me by surprise with great frequency.' ALAN TURING

Computers of the Second World War

ABOVE: *Alan Turing and his team built a machine called the Bomb to help crack the German codes created by the Enigma machines. The Bomb consisted of a series of dials (pictured), which allowed them to work through thousands of different combinations.*

BELOW: *These are electromagnetic counters from the Harvard Mark I computer, used to store the numerical information that was input. There were over 750,000 parts to the Mark I, and it weighed a massive 8 tons.*

THE SECOND WORLD WAR MARKED A turning point in computer technology. More sophisticated machines were urgently needed to help with all aspects of warfare, from calculations and communications to code-breaking. In the period between 1939 and 1945, some of the greatest minds in mathematics and technology were brought together by the Allied governments to design and build machines that would help them win the war.

ELECTROMECHANICAL COMPUTERS

One of the most important computers built during the Second World War was the Harvard/IBM Mark I, or Automatic Sequence Controlled Calculator (ASCC), built in 1943 by Howard Aiken (1900–73). Aiken, who had been a commander in the US navy, referred to the machine as the 'Mark', a naval term used to distinguish between different versions of equipment; the ASCC also became known as the Harvard/IBM Mark I. Many of the computers that followed carried the 'Mark' designation.

Aiken had been trying to create a machine that could solve equations that were too complex to do by hand, but he was having problems with the traditional technology of vacuum tubes. These took time to warm up and blew out easily, so Aiken tried using a different kind of switching mechanism – electromechanical relays.

Aiken designed the ASCC using Babbage's principles, and the machine could add, subtract, divide and multiply. It could also recall and use the results of previous calculations. The ASCC used decimal figures, which are much more complicated for computers than binary code. The US navy used the ASCC from 1944, but computer technology was developing rapidly and even by this time, the ASCC was out of date.

ELECTRONIC COMPUTERS

The first fully electronic computer was invented by the American John V. Atanasoff (1903–95) and his assistant Clifford Berry (1918–63) at Iowa State

Fact

ASCC

The ASCC Harvard Mark I was programmed with punched tape. Data was entered on an electrical typewriter that made punched cards. The mechanical relays did the same job as today's transistors, but they were big, slow and noisy by today's standards – though for its time the ASCC was very fast. It took up to 12 seconds to do division, but other calculations were quicker. It weighed 35 tons, had a million parts, used about 800 km of wire, and was 2.43 m high and over 15 m long.

Key People

Konrad Zuse (1910–95) was a German aircraft engineer. In the 1930s, Zuse had been frustrated by the sheer number of calculations needed on his projects. So in 1936 he built a machine he called the Z1, to speed up the calculation process. This was the world's first digital computer. The Z1 was complex in design, though, and used metal sheets as switches, which proved to be unreliable. Zuse did not give up, though, and worked to improve the design. He completed the Z2 in 1939, and the Z3 in 1941. The Z3 worked well, and was capable of complex calculations. This was the first fully functional programmable computer. It was destroyed during the war, but was rebuilt in the 1960s, proving that it worked.

Despite Zuse's success, the German government in the Second World War showed little interest in his achievements, and his computers were never used as part of Germany's war effort. After the war, Zuse began work on the Z4, still trying to improve the capabilities and efficiency of his machines. Today, many scientists and historians regard Zuse as the father of the modern computer.

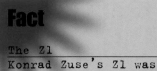

Fact

The Z1

Konrad Zuse's Z1 was about the size of a large table and was the first computer to use binary code. The Z1 converted decimal numbers into binary, and then used a program stored on punched tape to make the calculations. An output device showed the results in decimal form. An electric motor maintained the operation of the computer at 1 Hertz (1 cycle per second). Today's computers run more than a billion times faster than this.

University in the United States. Several versions were built between 1939 and 1942, each one an effort to improve on the last. The idea for these computers came about because Atanasoff was studying the structure of helium gas, and he wanted a machine that could help with the complex calculations involved with this research. The Atanasoff-Berry Computers (ABC) used binary code, had electrical switches called capacitors, and had separate memory and computational areas.

Although Atanasoff's computers were not programmable, their design was a major leap forward in computer science. The capacitors were constantly 'jogged' with electricity so that they remembered the binary digit that had been entered, in the same way that modern computer RAM remembers information. Atanasoff built a unit made up of vacuum tubes, which processed the data. This unit was a logic circuit: it obeyed the rules of binary arithmetic.

HOW DO COMPUTERS USE BINARY CODE?

A modern computer converts each letter or number on the keyboard into an eight-digit binary code of 0s and 1s. For example, the computer reads the 'A' key as 01000001 and translates it into a series of 'off' and 'on' electrical impulses – in this case off-on-off-off-off-off-off-on. The computer operator then sends the on/off impulses to a printer that produces the letter A.

Digital cameras and scanners work on the same principle. They instantly measure thousands of points of the different wavelengths of light reflected from an image and translate those measurements into a stream of binary sequences that trigger on/off electrical impulses. A single colour picture can take up more computer memory than all the words in three or four very long books!

Sound is also produced in waves. Again, a computer can measure thousands of points in a sound wave. And even though a three-minute song may consume ten times as much memory space as an image, today's computers process large amounts of data within seconds.

LEFT: *John V. Atanasoff (pictured here in 1983) built a series of ABC computers. These used binary code and were the first fully electronic computing machines.*

SECRET CODES

During the Second World War the German navy used an encryption device called Enigma to code all their messages. The operator typed in the orders for a submarine in the Atlantic, and Enigma encoded the message, using a very complicated system of mechanical rotors and wiring. This encoded message was then transmitted by radio to the submarine and fed into another Enigma machine for decoding by reversing the process.

The Germans believed the British could not decode the messages. For a while that was true. In 1941 German submarines sank huge numbers of British ships, and nearly won the war. Meanwhile, in 1940 the German army had started using another multi-rotor code machine called Lorenz. It encrypted messages using the five-bit binary system invented by Emile Baudot. Hitler sent messages to his battlefield commanders using Lorenz.

The British were desperate to crack the codes. A top-secret project named Ultra had been established at Station X, Bletchley Park, Buckinghamshire, in 1938. The same year, Polish agents had managed to

BELOW: *The Enigma cypher machine, used by the Germans during the Second World War to encrypt military messages.*

ABOVE: Teams of women trying to crack the code at Bletchley Park in 1942. Women often worked as code-breakers because so many men were away fighting in the war.

steal an Enigma machine from the Germans, providing vital evidence about how the code worked. Mathematicians and scientists were brought to Bletchley Park to use this captured evidence to develop techniques that would break the codes.

One member of the team was a young English mathematician named Alan Turing. He and his team were in charge of monitoring German transmissions and trying to translate the coded messages. To help

Key People

Alan Turing (1912–54) was a brilliant mathematician. In 1937 he published *On Computable Numbers,* a theory for how computers should work. The machines he outlined used programs and had a central processing unit. They read information on a series of 1s and 0s through a tape. This binary code described the steps that needed to be taken to solve a particular problem or perform a task. The computer would read and perform these steps in the correct order to reach the correct result. In this way, they were very like our modern computers. During the Second World War, Turing applied his extraordinary mind to cracking the Enigma code. After the war Turing continued to work in the new computer industry.

them with this, they built an electromechanical device, called the Bomb, which worked through all the combinations of letters until it found the right one for the day.

The Germans had books of daily codes and settings, and kept these with each Enigma machine. On 9 May 1941 the British navy captured an Enigma machine from a German submarine, along with the code books. With the help of these books, it was much easier to work out the settings for a particular day, but the process was still tedious and time-consuming. Despite this, by 1943 around 3,000 German messages were being decoded daily. Now the British and Americans knew where German submarines were and could attack them.

COLOSSUS

Experts at Bletchley Park knew how the German Lorenz cipher machine worked – the problem they had was deciphering the codes quickly enough to be able to act on the information they contained. A computer was the only answer. In 1943 the electronic digital 1,500-tube Colossus Mark I was built at Bletchley Park by a Post Office engineer called Tommy Flowers (1905–98). Flowers based Colossus on Alan Turing's 1937 theory of computers. Made of telephone-exchange parts, it took nearly a year to produce, and because the government doubted that Flowers could really make a workable machine like this, they would not fund the project and he ended up paying for a lot of it himself.

Flowers' self-confidence proved justified. Although the Mark I was not perfect, he continued to refine the computer, and in 1944 revealed the Colossus Mark II. This was so efficient that sometimes the British prime minister Winston Churchill and the American president Franklin D. Roosevelt were reading decoded German messages before the Germans for whom they were intended! Thanks to Colossus, when the Allies landed in France to drive the Germans out of the

Fact

ENIGMA
Enigma looked like a typewriter. The message was typed in, and an internal system of rotors changed each letter seven times. The rotors were altered and the machine rewired daily. The combination used was different for every letter, making 15 billion billion different combinations. The result was then transmitted by radio to, for example, a German submarine. On the submarine another Enigma machine reversed the process and reproduced the original message. To do this both machines' transmitter and receiver rotors and wirings had to be set up in the same way.

ABOVE: *They may have been small, but the Enigma machines used by the Germans in the Second World War could create codes from billions of combinations.*

RIGHT: Colossus was the first electronic programmable computer. Built at Bletchley Park, Colossus helped the code-breakers crack the Lorenz code, and enabled them to decipher secret German messages. This played a large part in helping Britain and its allies win the war.

BELOW: This is the receiver unit from ENIAC, the calculating machine that was later adapted to be used in research on the effects of the hydrogen bomb. ENIAC proved that high-speed digital computing was possible – even with the somewhat limited valve technology of the time.

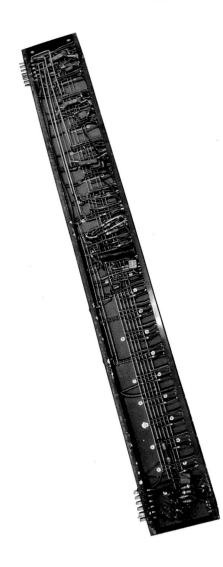

country in June 1944, they had huge amounts of information about the strength, positions and strategies of the German armed forces. Colossus is believed to have shortened the war by two years. By 1945 there were ten Colossus machines in operation, but they were destroyed after the war, and information about them was not revealed until 1989.

ENIAC

Because Colossus had to be kept a secret, it was an American machine called ENIAC that was credited as the first modern computer. Scientists in the United States had been working on a machine that would calculate where a shell would land after being fired, so that soldiers could position their guns correctly. The problem was that after a shell left the gun, forces such as air resistance and gravity acted on it, so that the path it followed (its trajectory) was curved rather than straight. The curve was different depending on what gun was used and at what angle it was placed, so many calculations had to be made to work out the trajectory of a shell. A computer would be able to do this much more quickly and accurately than a person could.

In 1943 the US Ordnance Corps paid the University of Pennsylvania to build an 'electronic numerical integrator and calculator' (ENIAC). Dr John Mauchly (1907–80) and John Presper Eckert (1919–95) were put in charge of the team that was formed to create such a machine. As it turned out, they did not complete ENIAC until after the war, but they helped establish the basic design of the circuits used by today's computers. In 1946 ENIAC was used for calculations in research on the first hydrogen bomb. It was later discovered that Mauchly had used information and designs originally drawn up by John V. Atanasoff for his ABC computers.

Fact

COLOSSUS VERSUS ENIAC

The Colossus Mark II used 2,400 vacuum tubes, and had eight racks about 2.3 m high, filling a large room. It was programmed through a system of switches. Colossus was very fast – it could process 5,000 encrypted characters every second. It could also print out decoded messages. Even modern computers are not much quicker than this!

ENIAC used 18,000 vacuum tubes, 1,500 relays, and weighed 27 tons. It consumed huge amounts of electrical power. Only the punched-card input and output devices were mechanical. ENIAC worked on electrical pulses and as a result it was fast and efficient – around 1,000 times faster than Howard Aiken's ASCC. However, it only processed decimal numbers, not binary digital code. Like Colossus, the processing was electronic and programming was done by switches.

The fact that both these machines could be programmed set Colossus and ENIAC apart from earlier computers.

BELOW: *Technicians wiring the massive ENIAC, the first general-purpose calculator, begun in Pennsylvania in 1943 and intended to be used in calculations of the flight of shells from weapons.*

CHAPTER FIVE

'The great thing about a computer notebook is that no matter how much you stuff into it, it doesn't get bigger or heavier.' **BILL GATES**

Towards Miniaturisation

ABOVE: *The Ferranti Mark I was one of the first commercially available computers. However, it did not prove very successful – computers were still a foreign language for most people and so programming the Ferranti was too difficult for those who bought the machines. This photograph shows engineers working at the computer in 1951.*

THE WAR YEARS HAD SEEN GREAT ADVANCES in computer technology. After the war, a whole new industry emerged based on developing this technology. One of the main problems with the computers that existed was that they were enormous and had thousands of working parts, which meant there were lots of things that could go wrong. There had to be a way of making computers smaller and more efficient.

ESTABLISHING PRINCIPLES

The first key principle that scientists worked on was programming. Although Colossus and ENIAC had been programmable, the information was stored on punched tape or cards. It would be better if programming information could be stored in a more permanent way.

Taking ENIAC as their starting point, John Mauchly and John Presper Eckert began work on a new computer they called EDVAC (Electronic Discrete Variable Computer), which was completed in 1947. Two years previously, John von Neumann (1903–57), professor of Mathematics at Princeton, had written a report on EDVAC, in which he suggested that binary code should be used for writing programs and for processing, because it was much simpler for the machine to understand. He also advised that computers store programs in a memory to speed them up.

Taking this advice, Mauchly and Eckert built UNIVAC (Universal Automatic Calculator), which went into service with the US Census Bureau. UNIVAC did away with punched cards and instead used programs stored on magnetic metal tape. Other tapes were used to input data and to record results. In 1952 UNIVAC processed voting data and correctly predicted that Dwight Eisenhower would win the US presidential election.

Similar techniques were being used in England to develop more efficient computers. A team at Manchester University created the Manchester Mark I computer in 1948. This was the first computer to store programs on a magnetic drum – a forerunner of today's hard drives. It was developed into a commercial version called the Ferranti Mark I in 1951, but it was not ideal for commercial use because it was extremely difficult to program. Later, an easier but slower programming language was designed for the machine.

Meanwhile, at Cambridge, Maurice Wilkes (b. 1913) was addressing the question of memory. He built EDSAC (Electronic Delay Storage Automatic Calculator). EDSAC used an early form of ROM; it contained information about the programs it used and was able to load them every time the machine was switched on, so the information did not have to be input time and again.

LEFT: *John Presper Eckert demonstrates how UNIVAC works to the director of the US census and local officials in 1951. UNIVAC could do calculations in half an hour that had previously taken three or more days.*

Fact

MAGNETISM IN COMPUTERS

Magnets have two poles: north and south. A north pole and a south pole are attracted to each other, but two north poles or two south poles will repel each other. In a computer, electrical pulses are turned into magnetic signals. Tiny particles of magnetic metal placed on tape can be forced into different positions using a magnet, and the magnetic signals produced can be recorded. The process can be reversed so that the signals on the tape are turned back into electrical pulses. Today, this process is used to record data on to disks and hard drives.

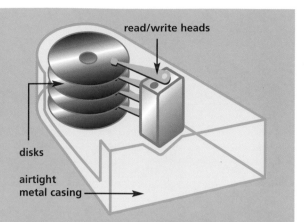

ABOVE: The hard disk of a computer stores information through magnetism. The north and south poles of the magnet correspond to the 0s and 1s of binary data. The hard disk moves round and an electromagnet in the read/write head at the end of the metal arm changes the disk's magnetism, writing information on to it.

THE FIRST MASS-MARKET COMPUTER

Until the 1950s IBM had concentrated on designing calculators, clocks and typewriters for businesses. When the US Census Bureau bought UNIVAC, however, IBM realised that computers were going to be big business and began to design its own machines. In 1952 it released the IBM 701 and in 1953 the 650. These took computers into a new era.

The principle of the 701 and 650 was that they came in units that were much easier to transport and install, and used magnetic plastic tape or punched cards. They could be used for different jobs in different places. In the end 1,800 650s were sold. This might seem very few by today's standards, but in the 1950s it was a huge advance, and made the 650 the world's first mass-market computer. Now different types of business were using computers for tasks such as managing staff payrolls.

Computers were still too big and expensive for smaller companies, though, and the idea of a home computer was science fiction. However, in 1946 a development had been

RIGHT: This punched card from the IBM 701 made the news in 1954: it was the first time an electronic 'brain' had translated information into English from another language – in this case Russian.

ABOVE RIGHT: The console of an IBM 360 series. These were the first computers to use transistors, making them much faster and more reliable.

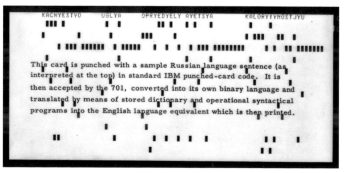

made that would revolutionise computers: the transistor. The transistor did everything a vacuum tube or electromechanical relay did, but it was a tiny package that used far less power and had no moving parts, so there was much less to go wrong. The first commercial transistors appeared in 1952.

By 1960 transistor-based computers had made the old types obsolete. In 1964 IBM introduced its transistorised System/360 series of computers, and all of them were much faster than their predecessors. There was a range of models, each of which was compatible with the others. The problem was that these new computers used new programs, and could not 'talk' to or share data with older computers, or with computers made by different companies.

GETTING SMALLER – THE CHIP

Computer research was very costly and a result of this was that computers were still expensive to buy. Only a few computer companies could survive in this small market. Those that did, like IBM, made huge profits, but if computers were to have a wider impact,

Fact

TRANSISTORS

Today, a transistor is made of layers of different types of silicon that conduct electricity in different ways, depending on the impurities in the metal. An electrical current carries the 0s and 1s of binary code in a series of off-and-on electrical pulses. Assembled in groups called logic gates, transistors can obey all the rules of binary arithmetic. The first transistors were made from pieces of germanium crystal, but today's silicon transistors are micro-scopically small, with millions assembled together in a micro-processor. They cost almost nothing to manufacture. If a modern mobile phone used vacuum tubes instead of tran-sistors it would be as big as several houses.

ABOVE: Transistors come in different sizes and are used in many devices. In today's computers millions fit on one microprocessor.

Fact

In 1965 an engineer called Gordon Moore (b. 1929) made a prediction, today called Moore's Law. He said the number of transistors in a single silicon chip would double every 18 months. This was pretty accurate – integrated circuits became more complex every year. In 1968 Moore co-founded the company Intel, which produced the first microprocessor, the Intel 4004. Compared to today's microprocessors the Intel 4004 was slow, but in 1971 it represented a leap into the future. With 2,000 transistors on a chip that measured just 3 mm by 4 mm it could do as much processing work per second as the 27-ton ENIAC, built just 25 years before. Today, one hundred million transistors in a microprocessor is common, equal to 41,666 Colossus computers!

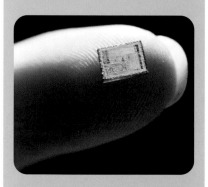

ABOVE: Today, a tiny chip like this can hold millions of transistors.

RIGHT: The printed circuit board revolutionised the computer industry. Placing all the transistors and circuitry on a board meant that the same device could be mass-produced and the cost greatly reduced.

they needed to be made much cheaper and smaller.

In 1960 the Digital Corporation produced a transistorised computer that was cheaper than IBM's machines. Customers had to write their own programs and do their own maintenance, but it still meant that more organisations could take advantage of computer technology. Universities, newspapers and schools bought Digital's machines and a whole series of models was produced. Computers were starting to find their way into everyday life. As they did, and as transistor-based products like radios and televisions became more common, transistors became cheaper.

Transistors were a brilliant idea, but each transistor had to be wired by hand, just as a vacuum tube or relay had. During the Second World War, the printed circuit had been invented, in which components were placed on a board where the 'wires' had been printed as strips of copper. In 1958, two engineers, Jack Kilby (b. 1923) and Robert Noyce (1927–90), independently invented the integrated circuit, basing it on printed circuit boards. In an integrated circuit, everything – including the wires and transistors – was etched on to a sheet of silicon. Identical integrated circuits could be made in vast numbers through mass-production, which meant they could be produced cheaply.

The integrated circuit made the microprocessor possible. In the late 1940s one transistor was the size of a packet of chewing gum. Today's computer microprocessors have hundreds of millions of transistors in the same space.

COMPUTER CHAOS

Early microprocessors were used in calculators. The microprocessors were still costly but the calculators were far cheaper than full-sized computers. Microprocessors were starting to play a part in small businesses, colleges and schools. They were small and cheap enough to be sold as part of packages. These included hobby computers like those made by Altair and Commodore, but there were many different types and they all worked differently. Users had to program the machines themselves and they all wrote different programs. Imagine if there were hundreds of different types of video player today, each using a different tape format. It would be impossible to share films, or to rent or buy tapes cheaply enough because no one could ever stock all the types. Now imagine that few of those computers had screens or storage systems. Programs were loaded from cassette tapes, and televisions had to be used as monitors. That is what it was like in the 1970s with computers: chaos.

Some of the first hobby computers were popular because they played simple electronic games. They appeared around 1972. Although games were of little use, they helped people grow accustomed to the idea of computers. Some of those who learned to program their machines went on to become commercial computer programmers and designers in the 1980s and 1990s.

STEPS FORWARD

IBM decided to take advantage of the multi-format chaos. In 1981 they designed a personal computer (PC) that came with the whole package: screen, keyboard, printer and floppy disk drive. Upgrades to a colour monitor and a hard drive were also available. IBM made the specifications public knowledge so that other manufacturers could copy them. Although this was risky, the gamble paid off, and IBM's design became the standard for computers.

The new computers came with a program called DOS (Disk Operating System). This operating system

BELOW: Two 8080 microprocessor chips, created in the 1970s for the Altair 8800. This was one of the first personal computers, and it proved so popular that the company could not keep up with the demand!

Key People

Bill Gates (b. 1955) is the founder of Microsoft – the largest and most successful computer software company in the world. Gates was fascinated by computers from an early age and began writing programs for them when he was only 13. Seven years later he started Microsoft, with his friend Paul Allen. At the time, computers were still large and unwieldly, and were certainly not widely available. Gates realised that computers could be a valuable tool for everyone, and so he began writing software for personal computers. Gates is still the chairman and chief software architect for Microsoft and his vision has not changed. Now that millions of people do have personal computers, his company concentrates on improving software, making it easier to use, cheaper and more fun.

Fact

HOME COMPUTERS

There was one step that revolutionised the home-computer market, and remarkably it was a step backwards. In the mid-1980s a British company called Amstrad packaged computer technology from the 1970s into their PCW (Personal Computer Wordprocessor). Supplied with screen, keyboard, printer, and a complete software package, it was considerably cheaper than IBM's PC or the Apple Macintosh, and provided an extremely functional computer for the home user. Although the machines were already obsolete, their price and usability brought many thousands of new customers into the home-computer market.

was the set of instructions the computer used to work, into which other programs such as word processors could be loaded. IBM bought DOS from a company called Microsoft, which was run by Bill Gates. Early versions of DOS were quite simple, but they have been constantly refined and other operating systems have been created. One of these was Microsoft Windows, the system used on most of the world's personal computers today. DOS was used on IBMs and also those computers that were copied by other manufacturers, called IBM-clones. What worked on one usually worked on other IBM-type computers. Although DOS is still used on some computers these days, it will soon become obsolete as better operating systems grow more widespread.

APPLE COMPUTER, INC

Steven Jobs (b. 1955) and Steven Wozniak (b. 1950) founded Apple Computer, Inc in San Francisco in the 1970s. Both men had been dabbling in computer design for several years, basing their ideas on the IBM machines that existed at that time. They decided that they could build a better type of computer, using an operating system they designed themselves. In 1976 they created the Apple I. In a market dominated by

IBM, which had been around for years, few people were interested in Apple's machine. This changed when they released the Apple II later the same year. This was the first self-contained and easy-to-use computer package. It all came in a plastic case and it had colour graphics. Despite a few teething problems, orders for Apple computers began to increase, and the problems were sorted out by the time the Apple Macintosh was released in 1984. The big advantage of Macs was that they were very user-friendly, and because they used an operating system designed especially for them, they worked more efficiently and with fewer errors. Of course, these new computers and the operating system they used were not compatible with the IBM-type computers and this remained a problem for many years. Today Apple's Power Mac can use the same software as IBM-type computers, but the divide between 'PCs' and 'Macs' still exists.

'There is no reason for any individual to have a computer in his home.'

KEN OLSEN, PRESIDENT OF DIGITAL EQUIPMENT, 1977

ABOVE: *The dramatic effects of computer miniaturisation over the past 25 years. The large disk is from one of the first IBM systems that had a disk drive (1984). It could hold 4 megabytes of information. The small disk is from a 1999 IBM PC. It can hold 6 gigabytes of information – around 1,500 times as much on a disk only a fraction of the size.*

BELOW: *The Apple Computer headquarters in Silicon Valley, California, USA – a far cry from Apple's humble beginnings, when Steven Wozniak and Steven Jobs ran the company from a garage.*

CHAPTER SIX

'The computer is only a fast idiot, it has no imagination; it cannot originate action. It is, and will remain, only a tool to man.'

AMERICAN LIBRARY ASSOCIATION

Computer Technology in the Twenty-First Century

ABOVE: *Computers help train pilots in a simulator.*

BELOW: *Tiny machines like this Global Positioning System – a navigation system using satellites – are controlled by computers.*

BY THE MID-1980S, THE MARKET WAS flooded with personal computers, and although the IBM Corporation had the lion's share, Apple Computers, Inc. was also doing extremely well. This was the boom time for personal computers. Computing power sped up and prices dropped. By 1990 a home computer sold for around about £800, with a 40-megabyte hard drive. By 2004 the same money bought a computer with an 80-gigabyte hard drive in a box the same size – this was 2,000 times as much storage.

CPUs

Computers have become much more useful to ordinary people because of programs like Microsoft's Windows. In the old days users had to program computers themselves. Nowadays all people have to do is install pre-programmed software on to the hard drives. The use of screen icons and other standard commands makes programs easy to start and use, especially now that instead of typing in instructions, a user can simply

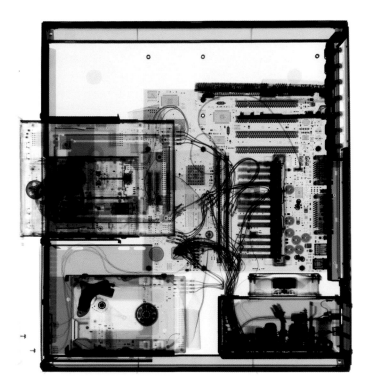

LEFT: This X-ray image of a standard desktop computer shows just what amazing technology is contained in a small unit. The CD-Rom drive is at centre left, transformers at bottom right. In the centre is the printed circuit board that houses the CPU and RAM chips. Ports at the far side are where input and output devices can be connected.

use the mouse to click on information on the computer screen to get things started. This 'point-and-click' technology made using computers much easier and more efficient. Also, many programs now work in a similar way and are compatible with one another. Data saved in a Windows-based program will usually be readable on most other Windows computers.

Today's CPUs can process so much information that home computers work as multimedia machines. They can operate complex games with detailed graphics and sound, play DVD movies, and process colour video. Computers today are a far cry from the computers of the 1930s and 1940s that were designed to do no more than process numbers.

COMPUTERS IN EVERYDAY USE

By 2000 governments, colleges, schools, businesses and many homes had abandoned old ways of recording data, writing letters and books, and processing photographs and sounds. Now it is even possible for people to work from home, but remain in touch with their workplace by being connected to their employer's network.

Computers have revolutionised our lifestyles. Online shopping, banking and booking holidays are just a few examples of what software compatibility and the Internet have made possible. Computers control satellite navigation systems, car security, supermarket food supplies, and even fly aircraft. Commercial airliners are managed by an enormous global database that coordinates all the flight schedules – without computers, there would be no international travel. Military organisations use computers for jobs as diverse

NETWORKING

Today's computers work easily in networks, where a number of machines are connected by cable or infrared links. They share information because the programs they use are the same, or at least compatible. A typical network in a business or school links dozens of computers in a Local Area Network (LAN). At the heart of a LAN is a larger and more powerful computer called a server. It can hold data and programs that all the other computers use. The ultimate network is the Internet. The Internet connects any computer with a modem or high-speed data link to the World Wide Web, allowing messages, files, images, documents, and programs to be shared in seconds all round the world.

as basic communications and systems that warn of a nuclear attack. Even in sport, computers have begun to play an important role, helping sportsmen and women improve their techniques through muscle-strength analysis and virtual practice sessions.

All this was science fiction in 1981 when the first personal computers became available, and unimaginable to Charles Babbage when he designed his calculating engines in the mid nineteenth century.

THE FUTURE

Every year brings huge advances in processing power and data storage. Computer manufacturers want to make money. New hardware needs new software to work. New software is written that needs new hardware. Individuals, businesses and governments are so dependent on computers they can easily find themselves having to upgrade regularly, often at vast expense. Never in history has new technology been made obsolete so quickly. Today, scientists are trying to create artificial intelligence: computers that can think for themselves.

Now that data can be transferred between computers so quickly, concerns have arisen about privacy and obscene material. Data-protection laws have been passed to protect the rights of individuals, but civil-rights

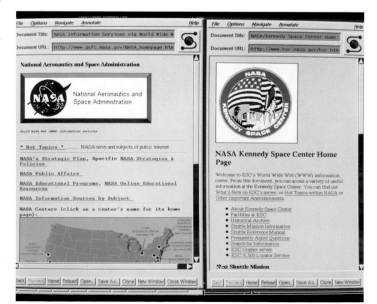

RIGHT: *The World Wide Web is the ultimate network. This 'information superhighway' allows communications and exchange of information at speeds that would have been unthinkable less than 50 years ago.*

'If we continue to develop our technology without wisdom or prudence, our servant may prove to be our executioner.'

GENERAL OMAR BRADLEY (US ARMY), ON THE RISE OF TECHNOLOGY AFTER THE SECOND WORLD WAR

groups have become concerned that governments can share data about people and monitor their behaviour. The exchange of child pornography on the Internet is now a major concern to police worldwide. Some software applications allow computer hackers to spread electronic viruses to any computer connected to the Internet. Hackers may also access the private records of computer users, including their credit-card numbers, financial data and other personal details. Meanwhile, 'spam' email swamps the Internet. People even fear that enemy countries or terrorists could explode a bomb that would set off an electromagnetic pulse (EMP). An EMP would destroy microprocessors, and with so many systems dependent on them today, the result would create chaos. These are problems that Charles Babbage and other computer pioneers never imagined.

Despite this, computers have made an extraordinary difference to our world. Who knows where technological progress will take us in the future?

ABOVE: *Computers have allowed great medical advances. Here, computers are used during a CAT scan to draw a kind of 'map' of the patient's body tissue to identify irregularities.*

TIMELINE

1613	Galileo publicises the Copernican theory that Earth and the other planets revolve around the Sun
1642	Blaise Pascal produces first mechanical calculator for addition and subtraction
1671	Gottfried Wilhelm Leibniz produces a mechanical calculator for addition, subtraction, multiplication and division
1703	Leibniz publishes his ideas about binary code as a pure form of logic because it represents only two, opposite, states: on and off
1804	Joseph Marie Jacquard's loom is introduced, using punched wooden cards to save labour and improve accuracy
1822	Charles Babbage publishes his plan for the Difference Engine
1871	Babbage dies, leaving the Analytical Engine unfinished
1874	Emile Baudot invents the first binary-code system for transmitting data
1876	Lord Kelvin creates the tide predictor
1890	US census data is sorted by Hollerith's census-counting machine
1906	Lee De Forest develops the vacuum tube
1930	Vannevar Bush builds the differential analyser
1937	Alan Turing publishes *On Computable Numbers*
1938–41	Karl Zuse builds the Z series – the first binary-code digital computers
1939	John V. Atanasoff builds the first binary-code electronic computer
1943	The Colossus computer is built to crack German codes; the Harvard Mark I (ASCC) is built by Howard Aiken
1945	John von Neumann sets out the principles of modern computing
1946	ENIAC is finished just after the end of the Second World War
1947	The transistor is invented; EDVAC is completed
1948	The Manchester Mark I is built
1949	EDSAC is completed at Cambridge
1951	UNIVAC becomes the first fully programmable computer, using magnetic tape; the Ferranti Mark I is the first commercially available computer
1959	The first solid-state transistor-based computer is IBM's Model 7090
1975	Bill Gates founds Microsoft
1976	Steven Jobs and Steven Wozniak found Apple Computer, Inc
1981	IBM produces the first personal computer
1984	The Apple Macintosh is introduced
1985	The Amstrad PCW is introduced
1993	Intel produces the first Pentium chip
1994	IBM and Apple produce the Power PC and Power Mac
1995	Windows 95, on which all later Windows systems are based, is released by Microsoft

GLOSSARY

BINARY A method of counting using two digits, 0 and 1. Computers use and process numbers in binary code in all operations.

BIT A piece of binary data transmitted as an electrical pulse which is either off, written as 0, or on, written as 1, the basis of digital information. Bits are grouped together, usually in packages of eight, called bytes.

BOMB An electromechanical machine used to decipher the Enigma coded messages during the Second World War.

BYTE *See* bit.

CD Compact Disc; a plastic disk rotated at very high speeds in a computer's CD unit. The information is stored optically in peaks and troughs in the plastic, which the CD unit's laser interprets as binary numbers.

CPU Central Processing Unit; the microprocessor at the heart of today's computers.

DECIMAL Base 10 numbering (0–9) used in all normal day-to-day calculations; computers use binary (base 2 numbers).

DIFFERENTIAL ANALYSER A computer that can solve mathematical equations.

DVD Digital Versatile Disc; the principle is the same as a CD, but DVDs can store far more data, including full-length movies.

DYNAMO A device that converts mechanical energy into electrical energy.

ELLIPSE A flattened circle. Planets move round the Sun in elliptical orbits.

ENCRYPT To disguise a message by turning it into a code (cipher).

ENIAC Electronic Numerical Integrator and Calculator; built for the US Ordnance Corps, and finished in 1946 by John Mauchly and John Presper Eckert.

ENIGMA An encryption machine used by the German navy in the Second World War. A system of mechanical rotors and wiring converted letters into different letters, using 15 billion billion combinations.

GIGABYTE 1,024 megabytes, or 1,048,576 kilobytes; an 80-gigabyte hard drive therefore holds 80 x 1,024 (= 81,920) megabytes.

GIGAHERTZ Equal to 1 billion Hertz, a measurement of processing speed in a computer. One Hertz = one revolution per second.

HACKER Someone who gains unauthorised access to computer systems and steals or corrupts data.

HARDWARE The components of a computer: screen, keyboard, processor, disk drives etc.

HYPERTEXT The language used to write web pages; it contains information about formatting web pages, and also the bookmarks and hyperlinks that move users to different parts of the page, or to new pages.

INPUT DEVICE A component of a computer that allows the user to put data in. The keyboard and the mouse are the two most common input parts.

KILOBYTE 1,024 bytes; abbreviated to KB or K.

MAINFRAME The central main processing computer in a network, linked to terminals. Terminals can be in the same building or miles away, and they can all share the mainframe.

MEGABYTE 1,024 kilobytes, or 1,048,576 bytes. Abbreviated to MB.

MICROPROCESSOR A solid-state silicon chip with numerous microscopic transistors embedded in it (*see also* CPU).

MULTIMEDIA Computers capable of using many different media: sound, video from DVDs or TV signals, photographs etc.

OUTPUT DEVICE A component of a computer that returns information to the user. The monitor (screen) is the most common output device.

PROGRAM A set of instructions that allows a computer to do a particular job, for example word-processing. Programs are written in special languages by programmers, which computer users do not need to know.

RAM Random Access Memory; memory chip where data is stored by the computer while it is being processed.

RIBBON CABLE A flat cable in which the conductors are laid side by side.

ROM Read Only Memory; memory chip that stores information about the computer's configuration, hardware etc.

SOFTWARE Programs used on a computer.

SPAM Junk emails sent out in millions, usually offering unwanted services to people who did not ask to be sent such emails.

STORAGE DEVICES Floppy disks, CDs, DVDs and hard drives, all of which allow data to be stored permanently on them.

TRANSISTOR A solid-state component made of silicon, through which digital bits pass in different ways, depending on the transistor's design. Transistors are now microscopically small, but each does the job a vacuum tube was once used for. Inside every microprocessor are millions of transistors.

UNIVAC UNIVersal Automatic Calculator. Computer built in 1951 by John Mauchly and John Presper Eckert.

VACUUM TUBE A glass bulb sealed with a vacuum used as an amplifier, and as a switching device. Expensive and unreliable, vacuum tubes have been totally replaced by transistors.

VDU Visual Display Unit; a computer's screen or monitor.

VIRUS A rogue program designed to damage a computer. Normally transmitted through the Internet.

FURTHER INFORMATION

WEB SITES

www.microsoft.com/
The home page of Bill Gates' Microsoft Corporation gives information about all the latest developments in personal computer technology. You can also find information about its museum and the history of the company.

www.ibm.com/
IBM's web site offers information about the cutting-edge technology the company is developing at the moment, as well as facts about its history and the role it has played in some of the greatest technological achievements of the twentieth century, including space travel.

www.apple-history.com/
This web site gives lots of details about the Apple Computer Company, its history and the hardware and software it now produces.

www.eingang.org/Lecture/
A clear and fascinating on-line lecture on 'Computers: From the Past to the Present', including chapters on all the key developments, from ancient times to the present day, and with links to other sites of interest.

BOOKS

Charles Babbage by Neil Champion: Groundbreakers, Heinemann Library, 2000
Hi-Tech Inventions by Mary Packard: Children's Press, 2004
The Road Ahead by Bill Gates: Longman, 1999
The Story of Microsoft by Adele Richardson: Smart Apple Media, 2004
Thomas Alva Edison by Brian Williams: Groundbreakers, Heinemann Library, 2000
Turing and the Computer by Paul Strathern: Big Idea, Arrow, 1997
Turing and the Universal Machine: The Making of the Modern Computer by Jon Agar: Revolutions in Science, Icon Books, 2001

INDEX